EDWARD HOPPER

EDWARD HOPPER

by Gail Levin

CROWN PUBLISHERS, INC. - NEW YORK

Title page: SELF-PORTRAIT, c. 1904
Oil on canvas, 20″ × 16″ (50.8 × 40.6 cm)
The Thyssen Bornemisza Collection, Lugano, Switzerland

Collection published under the direction of:
MADELEINE LEDIVELEC-GLOECKNER

Library of Congress Cataloging in Publication Data
Levin, Gail, 1948–
    Edward Hopper.

    1. Hopper, Edward, 1882–1967.
ND237.H75L48   1984   759.13   84-9488
ISBN O-517-55408-9

SOIR BLEU, 1914. Oil on canvas, 36″ × 7″ (91.5 × 183 cm)
Whitney Museum of American Art, New York. Bequest of Josephine N. Hopper

Edward Hopper (1882–1967) is recognized as the foremost realist painter of twentieth-century America. Proponents of abstract art also admire his work, for its composition, form, and light. Hopper was not a narrative painter and had long transcended his own early work in illustration. He painted all his watercolors as direct pictorial records of what he saw. In his oil paintings, however, he eventually synthesized his observations and, through his imagination, created much more than representations of reality. His spare compositions shunned unnecessary details and his subjects subtly suggested symbolic content but never confirmed it. Hopper's vision of life, as expressed in his view of his American surroundings, has a timeless quality that appeals today to a growing audience responding to the universal nature of his work. More than any of his contemporaries, Hopper captured the alienation of twentieth-century man.

Edward Hopper was a private man who chose to conceal his personal life. Shy and reserved, he usually preferred to hide behind a controlled public image of an independent, self-made painter, working in the narrow bounds of the American realist tradition without imposing on his art any intellectual or private content. He carefully limited his public image even to Lloyd Goodrich, his most important critical supporter and the organizer of his two major retrospectives in 1950 and 1964. Hopper never told Goodrich that he had studied with the

Self-Portrait, 1903. Charcoal on paper, 18½" × 12" (47 × 30.5 cm)
National Portrait Gallery, Smithsonian Institution, Washington, D.C.

then out-of-fashion William Merritt Chase, nor did he reveal anything of his long career as an illustrator. He insisted upon the cooperation of his sister, Marion, in keeping up his public image, which was carefully orchestrated by his wife, Jo. In 1956, when he was being interviewed for a «Time» magazine cover story, Hopper wrote to Marion that the researchers had «probed quite enough» and warned that if reporters tried to interview her, she should «tell them absolutely nothing about me or our family.»* Despite Hopper's reluctance to reveal himself, clues to his true nature are evident in the occasional interviews he gave, in his letters and those of his wife, in the large body of unexhibited work stretching from his childhood drawings to his last sketches, and in the comments in his record books and in the diaries, memoirs, and reminiscences of those who know him.

Woman with Umbrella, 1904
Pencil on paper, 9½" × 5½" (24.1 × 14 cm)
Achenbach Foundation for Graphic Arts.
The Fine Arts Museum of San Francisco.
Gift of Mr. and Mrs. John D. Rockefeller 3rd

THE FORMATIVE YEARS

When Elizabeth Griffiths Smith and Garrett Henry Hopper married in 1878, they lived with her widowed mother, Martha, in the small Hudson River town of Nyack, New York, in a house built in 1857 by Elizabeth's father, John Dewitt Smith. The Hopper's daughter, Marion, was born in 1880 and their son, Edward, arrived on July 22, 1882. In 1890 Garrett Hopper, a reluctant businessman, moved his dry-goods store to South Broadway, a short walk from the family home. The Hoppers' life was solidly middle class. They attended the local Baptist church (founded by Elizabeth Hopper's grandfather, Joseph W. Griffiths, in the middle of the nineteenth century). The children went to the local private school for the primary grades and to the church for Sunday school. Elizabeth Hopper appears to have taken great interest in her children's intellectual development. She introduced them to art and to the theater. Both Marion and Eddie, as he was called, drew from an early age, and Elizabeth Hopper saved much of Eddie's work and some of Marion's. The blackboard he received for Christmas at the age of seven became his first easel. He began to sign and date his precocious drawings by the age of ten, for, as one journalist reported, «the urge to draw had always been strong in him.»** Hopper's relationship to his surroundings was visual rather than

* Edward Hopper to Marion Hopper, letter of August 24, 1956. Copies of all letters cited are in the Hopper Archives, compiled by Gail Levin for the Whitney Museum of American Art, New York. The interview appeared in «The Silent Witness,» *Time*, 68 (December 24, 1956), pp. 28, 37–39.
** Bernard Myers, ed., « Scribner's American Painters Series: No. 7— "Deck of the Beam Trawler Widgeon," by Edward Hopper,» *Scribner's Magazine*, 102 (September 1927), pp. 32–33.

The Family, 1906–07
Pencil drawing
Collection: Mr. and Mrs. Mortimer Spiller, Buffalo, New York

Le Pont Neuf or Écluse de la Monnaie, 1909
Oil on canvas, 23¼″ × 28¾″ (59 × 73 cm)
Whitney Museum of American Art, New York
Bequest of Josephine N. Hopper

verbal. Throughout his life he avoided social interaction.   Hopper once described his father as « an incipient intellectual who never quite made it.» * As a youth, Eddie read avidly from his father's library — « the English classics and a lot of French and Russian in translation.» He recalled his father's sympathy with his artistic hopes, yet told how Garrett Hopper urged him to break away from the books he was constantly reading and go outside into the fresh air. Hopper's preference for solitude began at about the age of twelve when he suddenly grew to six feet in height, and no doubt felt awkward and different from his contemporaries.

The Hoppers' home was located at the top of a hill, with a clear view of the Hudson River, only one block away. During his boyhood, when Nyack was a prosperous port town with a thriving shipyard that built racing yachts, Hopper developed what was to become a lifelong passion for the sea and nautical life. Once Hopper's father, concerned about his son's apparent preference for solitude, bought him wood and tools and encouraged him to build a sailboat. Hopper was about fifteen when he finally built the boat, but as he later recalled « It wasn't very good. I had put the centerboard well too far aft and she wouldn't sail upwind very well.» Still, a career as a naval architect appealed to him, and during his youth he sketched many ships.

In 1899, after graduating from high school in Nyack, Hopper traveled daily to New York City to study illustration at the Correspondence School of Illustrating on West Thirty-fourth Street. His parents did not object to his becoming an artist, but they persuaded him to study commercial illustration, which offered a more secure income than did painting. The next year he enrolled at the New York School of Art on West Fifty-seventh Street. He remained there until 1906, studying with William Merritt Chase, Kenneth Hayes Miller, and Robert Henri.

The influences of his different teachers are often difficult to distinguish in the experimental, unresolved paintings of Hopper's student period. All the oils from this period, including a series of self-portraits, are dark and thickly painted (see title page). He frequently worked from the life and costume models at the school and often portrayed his classmates at work. As with most young artists undergoing a time of searching, his work reflected a variety of influences. In his later years Hopper generously praised Robert Henri as a teacher, but not as an artist. While he did not imitate much from Henri's style, he did work in the dark tones recommended by his teacher to better render mood and atmosphere. More than teach a specific style, Henri gave his students a philosophy. Hopper wrote that Henri's « courage and energy» did much to « shape the course of art in this country,» and claimed that « no single figure in recent American art has been so instrumental in setting free the hidden forces that can make the art of this country a living expression of its character and its people.» **

Hopper must have had high expectations upon leaving art school. At the New York School of Art, his talent was rewarded with prizes and scholarships and, eventually, with the opportunity to teach Saturday classes. In 1904, Hopper's sketch of a female model posing with an umbrella was among the student works reproduced in a magazine article about the

*   William Johnson, unpublished account of his interview with Edward Hopper, October 30, 1956. The next two quotations are also from this source.
** Edward Hopper, « John Sloan and the Philadelphians, » *The Arts*, 11 (April 1927), pp. 174–75.

On the Quai: The Suicide, 1906–07 or 1909
Conté, wash and touches of white, 17¹/₄" × 11¹¹/₁₆" (44.5 × 37.3 cm)
Whitney Museum of American Art, New York. Bequest of Josephine N. Hopper

SQUAM LIGHT, 1912. Oil on canvas, 24″ × 29″ (61 × 73.7 cm)
Private collection

School (see page 7). Two of Hopper's classmates, Rockwell Kent and Guy Pène du Bois, recalled his precocious talent in their memoirs. But even a modest degree of success would be a long time in coming.

In the decade following art school, Hopper worked mostly out of doors. Only later would he begin to experiment with composing oils in the studio through a process of improvisation, often loosely based on memories and sketches, but in the end imaginary. This method of combining observation and imagination dates back to his early training with Henri. In his most original conceptions, Hopper conveyed an authentic sense of mood, which again recalls Henri's advice to his students: «Low art is just telling things, as, "There is the night." Hight art gives the feel of night. The latter is nearer reality although the former is a copy.»* Here one is reminded of Hopper's subsequent fascination with the «feel of night,» as in his etching *Night Shadows* of 1921 and his well-known painting *Nighthawks* of 1942 (see pages 80 and 81). Having heard Henri, his favorite teacher,

Un Maquereau, study for « Soir Bleu », 1914
Conté on paper, 10" × 8⅜" (25.5 × 21.3 cm)
Whitney Museum of American Art, New York.
Bequest of Josephine N. Hopper

praise the work of European artists such as Degas, Manet, Renoir, Rembrandt, and Goya, Hopper traveled to Europe in order to see for himself the works of these great masters. He left for Paris in October 1906 and did not return until the following August. Through the Baptist church in Nyack, his parents arranged for him to board with a French family—a widowed mother and her two teenage sons—at 48 Rue de Lille, a building owned by the Eglise Evangélique Baptiste. Years later Hopper recalled: «I could just go a few steps and I'd see the Louvre across the river. From the corner of the Rues de Bac and Lille [sic] you could see Sacré-Cœur. It hung like a great vision in the air above the city.»** In a letter to his mother written soon after his arrival, he told of his delight with Paris:

> Paris is a very graceful and beautiful city, almost too formal and sweet
> to the taste after the raw disorder of New York. Everything seems to
> have been planned with the purpose of forming a most harmonious whole,
> which certainly has been done.***

*   Robert Henri, « The Art Spirit, » edited by Margery Ryerson (Philadelphia: J. B. Lippincott, 1923), pp. 274–75.
**   Quoted in Brian O'Doherty, « Portrait: Edward Hopper, » *Art in America*, 52 (December 1964), p. 73.
*** Edward Hopper to his mother, letter of October 30, 1906. The next quotation is also from this source.

The physical beauty of Paris captured Hopper's imagination; so did the Parisians: «Every street here is alive with all sorts and conditions of people, priests, nuns, students, and always the little soldiers with wide red pants.» He was particularly fascinated by the street life and cafés and by the Parisians' apparent hedonism:

> The people here in fact seem to live in the streets, which are alive from morning until night, not as they are in New York with that never-ending determination for the «long-green,» but with a pleasure-loving crowd that doesn't care what it does or where it goes, so that it has a good time.*

Still, Hopper's somber temperament led him to observe the tragic side of Parisian life, recorded in his poignant sketch *On the Quai: The Suicide* (see page 11). Hopper's art education in Paris came informally from visits to museums and exhibitions. It was at the Salon d'Automne in 1906 that he had his first extensive exposure to Courbet and Cézanne. The Salon featured a retrospective of thirty works by Courbet, including the artist's copy after Frans Hals's *Malle Babbe*, which Hopper himself had copied as an art student. Later Hopper listed Courbet among the artists he most admired and contrasted his work with that of Cézanne (represented in the Salon by ten works), which he felt lacked substance. Hopper also had his first opportunity to see paintings by Albert Marquet and Walter Richard Sickert, whose works bear some affinity to his own. Several American artists exhibiting in the Salon probably also caught Hopper's attention: Max Weber, Maurice Sterne, and Patrick Henry Bruce, his former classmate in New York, who had settled in Paris early in 1904. Although the Salon was a disappointment to Hopper—«for the most part very bad,» he wrote his mother, yet «much more liberal in its aims than the shows at home»**—it provided him with the firsthand knowledge he was seeking in Paris.

During that cold and rainy autumn in Paris, Hopper could not paint outdoors, as he preferred. As a result, his initial city scenes were dark, matching both his visual impression of his surroundings and the palette he had favored as a student in New York. The stylistic interests Hopper developed during his stay reflect his traditional training under Chase and Henri, his reticence to socialize with other artists, and his friendship with his former classmate, Bruce, whom he later acknowledged had introduced him to the work of the Impressionists in Paris: Sisley, Renoir, and Pissarro. In response, Hopper gradually lightened his palette and painted with broken brushstrokes. His favorite subjects were landscapes painted along the Seine. He did not, however, meet any of the avant-garde who were soon to influence Bruce. «I had heard of and knew about Gertrude Stein, but I wasn't important enough for her to know me.»*** While Hopper was later embarrassed at having so eagerly absorbed the influence of French art, he also wanted to make clear his early and consistent disregard for modernism.

---

* Edward Hopper to his mother, letter of November 23, 1906.
** Edward Hopper to his mother, letter of October 20, 1906.
*** William Johnson, unpublished account of his interview with Edward Hopper, October 30, 1956.

After a brief tour of London, Amsterdam, Haarlem, Berlin, and Brussels, Hopper returned to New York, where he worked as an illustrator. As he distanced himself from the impact of the Impressionists in Paris, Hopper darkened his palette once again and painted in a style closer to that of his former classmates, their teacher Robert Henri, and other contemporary realists, including John Sloan and George Luks. Silhouettes and the curvilinear forms of Art Nouveau characterize his illustrations of this period. Hopper went back to Paris from March through July 1909 and resumed painting along the Seine. The works he produced during this trip hint at the structural solidity that would characterize his mature painting; they demonstrate the development of light and shadow as dramatic vehicles and Hopper's awareness of the ability of light to convey a sense of immediacy and vitality. At this time, Hopper began to use a more consistently subdued palette, turning away from the high-key pastel colors he had employed in Paris during 1907. He also abandoned the short choppy

The Bullfight, c. 1917. Etching, second state, 5" × 7" (12.8 × 17.8 cm)
Private collection

Illustration for Carroll D. Murphy,
« What Makes Men Buy? »
System, The Magazine of Business,
22 September 1912, p. 231

"That was the best piece of news I could learn."

« That was the best piece of news
I could learn. »
Illustration for « Tales from the Road, »
Associated Sunday Magazine,
24 May 1914, p. 12

NEW YORK CORNER (CORNER SALOON), 1913
Oil on canvas, 24″ × 29″ (61 × 73.7 cm)
The Museum of Modern Art, New York
Abby Aldrich Rockefeller Fund

17

Les Poilus, 1915–17
Etching, 6″ × 7″ (15.2 × 17.8 cm)
Whitney Museum of American Art, New York
Bequest of Josephine N. Hopper

◁
Les Deux Pigeons, 1921
Etching, 8½" × 10" (21.6 × 25.4 cm)
The Metropolitan Museum of Art, New York
Harris Brisbane Dick Fund

Aux Fortifications, 1923
Etching, 12" × 15" (30.5 × 38 cm)
The Metropolitan Museum of Art, New York
Harris Brisbane Dick Fund

GIRL AT SEWING MACHINE, c. 1921
Oil on canvas, 19″ × 18″ (48.3 × 45.7 cm)
The Thyssen Bornemisza Collection, Lugano, Switzerland

20

East Side Interior
1922
Etching, 8" × 10"
(20.3 × 25.4 cm)
The Metropolitan
Museum of Art
New York
Harris Brisbane
Dick Fund

Evening Wind, 1921
Etching, 7" × 8⅜"
(17.8 × 21.3 cm)
The Metropolitan Museum
of Art, New York
Harris Brisbane Dick Fund

22

brushstrokes so notable in the 1907 Paris canvases. Typical of 1909 is the dark-toned color scheme of *Ecluse de la Monnaie*, which reflects Hopper's fascination with the play of sunlight and cast shadows (see page 9).

Hopper earned enough money from his commercial work to make a third and last trip to Europe, in May 1910. After spending a few weeks in Paris, he departed for a long-anticipated trip to Spain—to Madrid, where he saw a bullfight, and to Toledo, which he described as « a wonderful old town. »* The drama of the bullfight deeply affected him—he would later make both an illustration and an etching on this theme (see page 15).

> The killing of the horses by the bull, he wrote, is very horrible, much
> more so as they have no chance to escape and are ridden up to the bull
> to be butchered . . . the entry of the bull into the ring however is very
> beautiful; his surprise and the first charges he makes are very pretty.*

Returning to France, Hopper spent another few weeks in Paris and on July 1, 1910, sailed for New York. Although he never again visited Europe, his memories remained vivid and the experience had a significant impact on his later development.

The next few years were a period of esthetic and economic struggle for Hopper. In New York, where by late 1913, he settled permanently into a studio at 3 Washington Square North, he continued to paint reminiscences of Paris. Years later he admitted, « It seemed awfully crude and raw here when I got back. It took me ten years to get over Europe. »** And as late as 1962, he insisted, « I think I'm still an Impressionist. »*** Along with producing commercial advertisements, Hopper began illustrating for several periodicals— « Sunday Magazine, » « The Metropolitan Magazine, » « Everybody's, » and « System, The Magazine of Business. » In his first illustrations for « Everybody's » and « System » (see page 16), in 1912, Hopper developed his pictorial conceptions much beyond the simple emblematic ads he had produced earlier. His French experience had changed his illustrations as it had his paintings. Some of his magazine designs are related compositionally to the art of the American expatriate James McNeill Whistler, and to that of Degas and other French Impressionists. Although Hopper accepted illustration as a means to support himself, he found the work exasperating:

> Partly through choice, I was never willing to hire out more than three
> days a week. I kept some time to do my own work. Illustrating was
> a depressing experience. And I didn't get very good prices because I
> didn't often do what they wanted.****

*   Edward Hopper to his sister, letter of June 9, 1910.
**   Quoted in O'Doherty, « Portrait: Edward Hopper, » p. 73.
***   Quoted in Katharine Kuh, « The Artist's Voice, Talks with Seventeen Artists » (New York: Harper & Row, 1962), p. 135.
**** Quoted in Suzanne Burrey, « Edward Hopper: The Emptying Spaces, » *Arts Digest*, April 1, 1955, pp. 9 and 33.

ROCKS AT THE FORT, GLOUCESTER, 1924. Watercolor, 13¾″ × 19¾″ (35 × 50.2 cm)
Collection· Mr. and Mrs. Alvin L. Snowiss

Both Hopper's frustration at having to earn his living in this way and his love of everything French are documented by a humorous sign he made in French, captioned «Hopper Maison Fondée 1882» («House of Hopper, Founded 1882» — the year of his birth).

> Maison E. Hopper. Objects of art and utility. Oil paintings, engravings, etchings, courses in painting, drawing and literature, repairing of electric lamps and windows, removal and transportation of trunks, guide to the country, carpenter, laundry, hair dresser, fireman, transportation of trees and flowers, marriage and banquet rooms, lectures, encyclopedia of art and science, mechanic, rapid cures for the ill in spirit such as flightiness, frivolity and self-esteem. Reduced prices for widows and orphans. Samples on request. Demand the registered trademark. Maison E. Hopper, 3 Washington Square.

Hopper spent the summer of 1912 in the seacoast town of Gloucester, Massachusetts, painting with Leon Kroll, a contemporary who had also lived in Paris. Along the picturesque waterfront and rocky shore of Gloucester, where American artists had been painting since the middle of the nineteenth century, Hopper's boyhood enchantment with the nautical world he had known on the Hudson River reasserted itself. But the experimental formal concerns

The Monhegan Boat, 1918
Etching, 7" × 9"
(17.8 × 22.8 cm)
The Art Institute
of Chicago
Gift of the Print and
Drawing Club

that had characterized his painting of the last few years continued. In *Squam Light*, painted on Cape Ann near Annisquam, he worked at rendering solid forms with emphatic lights and shadows (see page 12). The following January, Hopper exhibited *Squam Light* and one of his Paris pictures, *La Berge*, in an artist-sponsored group show at the MacDowell Club in New York. Neither painting sold.

In February 1913 Hopper entered one oil painting, *Sailing*, in New York's International Exhibition of Modern Art, familiarly known as the Armory Show. He had been invited to participate by the Domestic Exhibition Committee, which requested that artists enter «works in which the personal note is distinctly sounded.» Despite the fact that avant-garde European art captured most of the attention and made the American works seem tame by comparison, Hopper's *Sailing* sold for $250. His first sale of a painting had great significance to him, and he was disappointed when it did not generate the sale of other works. Throughout the next decade Hopper continued to struggle financially, able to sell only his illustrations and prints—and those at very modest prices.

In February 1915, when Hopper again showed with a group at the MacDowell Club, critics analyzed his work for the first time. Hopper exhibited the monumental *Soir Bleu* of about 1914, and a much smaller canvas, *New York Corner* (see pages 5 and 17). *Soir Bleu*, one of the largest canvases he ever painted, represented a major achievement for Hopper and revealed his continuing involvement with French subject matter. Unfortunately, xenophobic

Night on the El Train, 1918
Etching, 7½" × 8"
(19 × 20.3 cm)
The Metropolitan Museum
of Art, New York
Harris Brisbane Dick Fund

critics dismissed it as only an « ambitious fantasy, » praising instead the small New York scene. *Soir Bleu* reflects Hopper's sentimental recollections of a world of romance and intrigue. Although he had know this world only as an observer on the periphery, it had fueled his imagination and left a lasting impression. Hopper's French experience remained with him all his life, symbolizing a romantic and exotic moment that he relived through his memories. To his mother, he described the « carnival » of Mi-Carême, which he explained was « one of the important fêtes of the year » :

> Everyone goes to the "Grands-Boulevards" and lets himself loose. . . . Do not picture these in costume, they are not for the most part . . . perhaps a clown with a big nose, or two girls with bare necks and short skirts. . . . The parade of the queens of the halles [markets] is also one of the events. . . . Some are pretty but look awkward in their silk dresses and crowns, particularly as the broad sun displays their defects — perhaps a neck too thin or a painted face which shows ghastly white in the sunlight.*

This letter helps explain the figures in *Soir Bleu* — the eerie look of the standing woman with her painted face and long neck, the presence of the clown, and the scant attire worn by the women. Hopper titled his sketch for the man on the far left, « Un Maquereau » (French slang for procurer), suggesting that the woman with the heavily painted face is a prostitute approaching prospective clients (see page 13). The café appears to be located on

* Edward Hopper to his mother, letter of May 11, 1907.

the outskirts of the city, along the old ramparts encircling Paris where people of the demimonde met to socialize. In representing the atmosphere of a celebration he remembered, Hopper was working in the tradition of the *fête galante*, a pictorial genre invented by Antoine Watteau in the eighteenth century, which explores the psychological subtleties of human nature without employing an overt story. Hopper's clown, dressed in white, recalls images of Pierrot, the pathetic figure from the commedia dell'arte. The strange woman with the painted face suggests a more recent inspiration — the ghastly colored face of the female in the right foreground of Toulouse-Lautrec's *At the Moulin Rouge* of 1892.

As Hopper distanced himself from the influences of his student period, his artistic range broadened. His later works cannot be attributed to one or two sources, but owe something to a variety of images, many of which he may not have consciously recalled. The composition

House on a Hill or *The Buggy, 1920. Etching, seventh state, 8″ × 10″ (20.3 × 25.4 cm) Philadelphia Museum of Art. The Harrison Fund*

HASKELL'S HOUSE, 1924. Watercolor, 14″ × 20″ (35.5 × 50.8 cm)
Private collection

Manhattan Bridge and Lily Apartments, 1926
Watercolor, 13½″ × 19½″ (34.3 × 49.5 cm)
Collection: Mr. and Mrs. Joel Harnett

30

RAILROAD CROSSING, 1926
Watercolor, 13½″ × 19½″ (34.3 × 49.5 cm)
Private collection

31

PROSPECT STREET, GLOUCESTER, 1928
Watercolor, 14″ × 20″ (35.5 × 50.8 cm)
Private collection

DAVIS HOUSE, 1926
Watercolor, 14″ × 20″ (35.5 × 50.8 cm)
Collection: Mr. and Mrs. Mortimer Spiller

BOW OF A BEAM TRAWLER, 1924
Watercolor, 14″ × 20″ (35.5 × 50.8 cm)
Collection: Mr. and Mrs. Malcolm Chace

GLOUCESTER HARBOR, 1926
Watercolor, 14″ × 19½″ (35.5 × 49.5 cm)
The Warner Collection of Gulf States Paper Co., Tuscaloosa, Alabama

HOUSE BY THE RAILROAD, 1925. Oil on canvas, 24″ × 29″ (61 × 73.7 cm)
The Museum of Modern Art, New York

of *Soir Bleu* is most closely related to Degas' *Women in a Café, Evening*, a pastel on monotype of 1877. Like Degas, Hopper boldly divided an oblong surface with a post, placed on the left, which cuts through the back of the profile of one figures's head. In both works, several habitués are seen in profile and from behind, seated in the foreground, spread across the entire horizontal composition; the round table tops tilt up with chairs placed at casual angles around them. Yet *Soir Bleu* is shallow, almost friezelike, only later, as in his 1942 *Nighthawks* (see page 81), would Hopper adopt Degas' deep, complex space as well. In their uncommunicative, introspective nature, the figures in *Soir Bleu* anticipate the figures that populate the paintings of Hopper's maturity. But Hopper did not immediately pursue this psychological approach. Instead, for the rest of the decade, he painted landscapes without figures and city scenes with only sketchy, diminutive figures resembling those in his *New York Corner*. He never again exhibited *Soir Bleu*, perhaps because of the negative critical reaction it received.

Hopper's enthusiasm for things French was also apparent in his etchings. He began to work with the medium in 1915, through his friend Martin Lewis, an Australian emigré who, like Hopper, worked in commercial art and illustration. Lewis had just started etching and

American Landscape, 1920
Etching, 7½" × 12½" (19 × 31.7 cm)
The Metropolitan Museum of Art, New York. Harris Brisbane Dick Fund

provided Hopper with technical advice and encouragement. Hopper's initial efforts were tentative, but he would soon master the process. He chose many French subjects for his etchings and even gave four prints French titles: *Les Poilus*, *La Barrière* (1915–18), *Les Deux Pigeons* and *Aux Fortifications* (see pages 18 and 19).

All of Hopper's oil paintings after the exhibition of *Soir Bleu* in 1915 have American themes. Twarted by the critics in his desire to depict the French themes he loved, Hopper apparently chose to relegate the French material to the smaller, less controversial medium. Although his prints were more readily accepted for exhibition and sold well at the modest prices he asked, from the beginning Hopper viewed himself as a painter, not as printmaker or an illustrator. Hopper once commented: « Etching? I don't know why I started. I wanted to etch, that's all. » [*] Even the juries at the National Academy of Design, that conservative institution which repeatedly rejected Hopper's paintings, recognized the masterly draftsmanship of his prints and regularly included them in exhibitions.

A turning point in Hopper's development occurred in January 1920, when he had his first one-man show — at the Whitney Studio Club — at the age of thirty-seven. Guy Pène du Bois, who organized the show, later recalled that it « was, curiously enough, composed entirely of pictures painted in Paris. » [**] Of the sixteen oil paintings exhibited, ten were painted in France over a decade earlier, one just after Hopper returned in 1909, and the remainder during the more recent summers spent in Massachusetts or Maine. Ignoring nationalist critics, Hopper now even listed the French titles in the catalogue, rather than the English translations he had used when he first exhibited three of the paintings in 1908. His decision to show primarily his French works indicates the high regard he still had for these pictures and the importance he placed on his stay in Paris. It may also reveal Hopper's frustrated efforts to achieve critical success. During the previous five years, the American theme paintings he had exhibited failed to receive critical praise, so perhaps, with Du Bois's encouragement, he tried the French works again in hope of achieving recognition. Lack of critical attention and sales forced Hopper to confront the failure thus far of his career as a painter.

In his etchings of about 1920, Hopper began to focus on the American vernacular architecture that would eventually be incorporated so successfully into his paintings. For example, the Victorian structure of his etching *House on a Hill* reappears in the view from the window in his 1921–23 painting *Moonlight Interior* (see pages 28 and 21). The conception of a solitary house by train tracks in his etching *American Landscape* stripped of distracting details such as trees and cows, became the essence of the stark drama in the 1925 painting *House by the Railroad* (see pages 37 and 36).

In *Night Shadows*, Hopper's etching of 1921, the unusual viewpoint is sharply from above, as if from an upper-story office across the street (see page 80). A solitary man is visible before the closed shops on the quiet corner lit eerily by street lamps, one of which casts a

[*] Quoted in O'Doherty, « Portrait: Edward Hopper, » p. 73.
[**] Guy Pène du Bois in « Juliana Force and American Art: A Memorial Exhibition » (New York: Whitney Museum of American Art, 1949), p. 44.

long shadow across the entire sidewalk. The man's shadow appears as a haunting presence, creating a surprising and disarming effect. Hopper's experiments with etching probably helped him approach compositional issues with a fresh intensity and refine his ideas into stronger, more personal designs. Producing etchings in the studio encouraged him to improvise both subject and composition—a creative process that he carried over into more of his oils. During the early 1920s, his mature painting style began to emerge, perhaps in part as a result of his experience as an etcher. Hopper himself later said: «After I took up etchings, my paintings seemed to crystallize.»* When Hopper etched his plates in his studio, he had to rely on memory or sketches. Thus, rather than work directly before his subject as he had in most of the early oils, he gradually began to invent his subject matter and composition in the studio. An etching such as *The Monhegan Boat* was based on recollection (see page 25). His mature oils eventually became realizations of imagined images or were developed from one or several simple sketches he made on location and synthesized in his studio. Since Hopper's career as an illustrator coincides with and encompasses the years he devoted to etching, it is not surprising to find relationships between the two endeavors. There are often common motifs and subjects, as well as similar compositional arrangements. These also appear in the paintings of his maturity. Yet while he later denigrated his illustrations, he remained proud of his etchings long after he stopped making them in 1923, even including some of them in his retrospectives in 1950 and 1964. After producing his last two drypoints in 1928, he abandoned prints entirely. Among the subjects that Hopper repeatedly chose for both his etchings and his illustrations were trains, boats, soldiers, figures in interiors, and urban street scenes. All these subjects reappear in his subsequent paintings.

As Hopper developed his mature style, he relied on several compositional formats which he continued to use throughout his career. These include a simple frontal view parallel with the picture plane, a scene viewed at an angle from above, and a subject placed on an oblique diagonal axis cutting into the picture's depth (see pages 42, 43, and 68). By the 1920s, Hopper also began to depict views through a window out to an exterior space (see page 22). As in romantic nineteenth-century art, the window symbolized the expansive world beyond but also served as a barrier separating the viewer-voyeur from the drama within. Hopper's youthful experiments with light had remarkable results for his mature style: through the skillful manipulation of light, shadow, and tone he learned to dramatize an entire composition. Whether the source is the sun or artificial illumination at night, the light is clearly defined and intense. In attempting to break new ground in his painting during the 1920s, Hopper found inspiration in John Sloan's interpretations of New York: «Sloan not having been abroad, has seen these things with a truer and fresher eye than most.»** He particularly admired the paintings and prints produced just after Sloan's arrival in New York from Philadelphia in 1904, exempting from his enthusiasm only «one or two of the large portrait etchings done without much show of interest.» Among his contemporaries, Hopper seems to have identified most closely with Sloan, who like himself had worked as an illustrator at the beginning of his career: «The hard early training has given to Sloan a facility and a power of invention that the pure painter seldom achieves.»

* Quoted in Burrey, «Edward Hopper: The Emptying Spaces,» p. 10.
** Hopper, «John Sloan,» p. 172. The next two quotations are also from this source.

More than anything else, Sloan's choice of subject matter made an impression on Hopper during his formative years. Many subjects, and even titles like *Night Windows* and *Barber Shop*, appeared first in Sloan's work and subsequently in Hopper's. Common themes include a woman in an interior by a window, city rooftops, urban street scenes, and city parks, restaurants, and movie theaters. Sloan's influence was one of several factors that contributed to Hopper's shift away from French subjects. Hopper's admiration for Sloan also contributed to his growing interest in the female figure. Earlier Hopper had experimented with drawings and etchings of a solitary woman in an interior setting. About 1921, he began to focus on female figures, either nude or in deshabillé, alone in domestic settings. In *Girl at Sewing Machine* (see page 20), a long-haired female wearing only a slip or gown concentrates on sewing, seemingly unaware that she has been observed by the artist. Hopper was perhaps influenced in these candid views by Sloan's *The Cot*, an oil painting of 1907, which he had seen in a 1908 exhibition of The Eight. From the 1910 Independents' Exhibition, he also knew Sloan's domestic interior *Three A. M.*, a scene of two women, one half-dressed, standing over a stove. Hopper's print *Evening Wind* of 1921 is related in mood to Sloan's 1905 etching *Turning Out the Light*. Sloan's print was rejected in 1906 by the Committee on Etchings of the American Water Color Society as too vulgar to be exhibited. Like Sloan, Hopper depicted a sensuous situation and dramatized the scene through light and shadow. He added the suggestive caress of the curtain blowing in, a device that he would use repeatedly and that he may have borrowed from films of the 1910s. Sloan, who chose his scenes by «night vigils at the back window,»* may have suggested to Hopper the expressive potential of a woman in an intimate setting, unaware of being observed. Hopper's *Moonlight Interior* of 1921–23 (see page 21), is close in mood and composition to his *Evening Wind* (see page 22). Both intimate scenes make the viewer a voyeur looking in at the lone nude woman as the wind suggestively disturbs the curtain at the window. In *Moonlight Interior*, Hopper effectively used a muted palette to convey the mood. He gives the viewer a glimpse not only of the woman unaware but, through the window, a gabled house in the moonlight, setting up an erotic tension between interior and exterior through the contrast of her soft curved body and the aggressive angularity of the architecture beyond. Here, Hopper has arrived at a theme he would continue to explore in his maturity.

While in Gloucester during the summer of 1923, Hopper began to paint watercolors of the local landscape and architecture. He was evidently encouraged to experiment by his friend Jo Nivison, who had already been exhibiting her own watercolors, some painted outdoors in Provincetown the previous summer. Both students of Henri and Miller, Nivison and Hopper had met at the New York School of Art, where Henri had painted a portrait of Nivison (*The Art Student*) in January 1906. Nivison and Hopper occasionally saw each other during summers spent in Ogunquit and on Monhegan Island. They had been included in the same group exhibition in December 1922 at the Belmaison Gallery at John Wanamaker's department store in New York and the following summer had gone to Gloucester, where they went on sketching trips together. Although of contrasting personalities, Nivison and Hopper shared many interests: both were well read, had traveled in Europe, loved the theater and poetry, and were romantic. Years later, Jo reminisced that Edward once «started quoting

---

* John Sloan, « Gist of Art, » (New York: American Artists Group, 1939), p. 220.

ADOBE HOUSES, 1925. Watercolor, 13⅝″ × 19⅝″ (35.2 × 50.5 cm)
Private collection

SUNDAY, 1926
Oil on canvas, 29″ × 34″ (73.7 × 86.4 cm)
The Phillips Collection, Washington, D.C.

EARLY SUNDAY MORNING, 1930
Oil on canvas, 35″ × 60″ (89 × 152.4 cm)
Whitney Museum of American Art, New York
Bequest of Josephine N. Hopper

43

TABLES FOR LADIES, 1930
Oil on canvas, 48¼" × 60¼" (122.5 × 153 cm)
The Metropolitan Museum of Art, New York
George A. Hearn Fund

44

CHOP SUEY, 1929
Oil on canvas, 32⅛″ × 38⅛″ (81.6 × 97 cm)
Collection: Mr. and Mrs. Barney A. Ebsworth

Verlaine on Bass Rock in Gloucester» and that she surprised him by taking it up when he stopped.*

That fall Jo was invited by the Brooklyn Museum to exhibit six of her watercolors in a group exhibition of American and European artists to be held there at the end of the year. She recalled: «I got over there and they liked the stuff and I started writing and talking about Edward Hopper, my neighbor. . . . They knew him as an etcher, but they didn't know he did watercolors.» ** Jo suggested that Edward «bring some of his things over for the show.» Six of his watercolors were accepted for the exhibition, where they hung next to hers. She also remembered that he «carried my stuff back when the time came... didn't have me hauling them through the subway—what a sorry sight I'd have made.» Jo's generous gesture in bringing Hopper's watercolors to the attention of the Brooklyn Museum proved to be significant for both of their careers. Except for illustrations and caricatures, Hopper had not used watercolor since his art school days. Juxtaposed against Hopper's work, which received rave reviews from the critics, Nivison's work was ignored, as it would be in the years to come. In December the Brooklyn Museum purchased *The Mansard Roof* for $100—Hopper's first sale of a painting since 1913.

Hopper used watercolor with a sense of confidence, improvising as he went along. He applied the pigments with only a faint pencil sketch, outlining the structures he intended to paint. What interested him was not the creation of textures or the manipulation of the medium but the recording of light. Hopper expressed the forms and views before him through the play of light and shadow. His watercolors were simply recordings of his observations, painted almost entirely out of doors, directly before his subject matter.

> At Gloucester when everyone else would be painting ships and the waterfront I'd just go around looking at houses (see page 29). It is a solid looking town. The roofs are very bold, the cornices bolder. The dormers cast very positive shadows. The sea captain influence I guess— the boldness of ships.***

Elated by his recent successes and no doubt appreciative of Jo's help and encouragement, Hopper entered a period of uncharacteristic optimism. On July 9, 1924, at the Eglise Evangélique on West Sixteenth Street in New York, shortly before his forty-second birthday, he and Jo were married. Their best man, Guy Pène du Bois, visited the Hoppers in Gloucester, where they went for the summer. Hopper produced more watercolors in Gloucester, and in November the Frank K. M. Rehn Gallery gave him his second one-man show—his first in a commercial gallery. All eleven watercolors in the exhibit and five additional ones were sold. The show was a critical success as well.

This exhibition was of special significance to Hopper's career, for he was finally able to give up his work as an illustrator and devote himself entirely to painting. He claimed to have

* O'Doherty, « Portrait: Edward Hopper, » p. 80.
** Josephine Verstille Nivison Hopper, interviewed with Edward Hopper by Arlene Jacobwitz at the Brooklyn Museum, April 29, 1966. The next two quotations are also from this source.
*** William Johnson, interview with Hopper, p. 17.

been a poor illustrator because he disliked the subjects demanded: « I was always interested in architecture, but the editors wanted people waving their arms. » * He also recalled: « Illustration didn't really interest me. I was forced into it in an effort to make some money. That's all. I tried to force myself to have some interest in it. But it wasn't very real. » ** By the time Hopper ended his career as an illustrator, he had created illustrations for short stories for « Scribner's, » « Adventure, » and other popular magazines, and for non-fiction articles for several trade and business publications including « Wells Fargo Messenger, » « The Morse Dry Dock Dial, » « Tavern Topics, » and « Hotel Management. » These trade periodicals required factual representations of offices, trains, hotels, ships, and so forth, and they probably offered Hopper more appealing subjects than those called for in the illustration of fiction.

One of the last magazine covers Hopper illustrated, for « Hotel Management » in June 1925 (see page 48) recalls Renoir's *The Luncheon of the Boating Party* of 1881. Hopper portrayed a similarly festive outdoor scene with relaxed men and women eating and drinking. Hopper's interest in Renoir was probably prompted by an exhibition of the artist's work at the Durand Ruel Galleries in New York in 1922 and by the subsequent attention paid to Renoir's *Luncheon* in the many articles on the exhibition. Even Hopper's pictorial devices — the diagonal axis for his tables seen from above and the placement of the two poles supporting a gaily striped scalloped awning — appear to owe a debt to Renoir's celebrated canvas. When Hopper gave up etching in 1923, he had became preoccupied with watercolor. Now his renewed sense of confidence after years of discouraging struggle prompted him to work more frequently in oil, tackling more ambitious canvases and working toward what would become his mature style.

In 1923 he enrolled in the evening sketch classes at the Whitney Studio Club, then located on West Eighth Street. For the modest fee of twenty-five cents he could sketch from the life model provided. Not long after their marriage, however, Jo insisted that she alone should pose for him, and for the rest of his life she modeled for all his female figures. Although his watercolors remained direct and spontaneous, Hopper's oil paintings became more carefully constructed. Eventually he composed them entirely in the studio, often drawing upon simple black-and-white sketches or even verbal notations on paper that he had made in several locations. If Hopper made sketches for most of his oils in the early 1920s, they have not survived. Nonetheless, the precise character of his compositions indicates thoughtful planning.

House by the Railroad marks what can be termed Hopper's artistic maturity (see page 36). He had at last resolved a large number of important influences, from Degas to Sloan, to create a personal style. In this skillfully constructed composition, a mansard-roofed Victorian house stands alone against the cutting edge of railroad tracks. The tracks cut slightly inward on a subtle diagonal to create a deeper space and a more powerful image, one of the most enduring symbols in American art. By 1925 this solitary Second Empire house from the nineteenth century already recalled America's more innocent past — a simpler time that has

---

* Edward Hopper, quoted in Archer Winsten, « Wake of the News. Washington Square North Boasts Strangers Worth Talking To, » *New York Post*, November 26, 1935.
** Quoted in O'Doherty, « Portrait: Edward Hopper, » p. 73.

BAPTISTERY OF SAINT JOHN'S, 1929
Watercolor, 13⅝″ × 19⅝″ (35.2 × 50.5 cm)
Private collection

Cover for « Hotel Management, 7 June 1925, » 8³/₄″ × 4¹/₁₆″ (22.3 × 10.4 cm)

been left behind by modern urban life and its complexities. Hopper's canvas suggests a glimpse back in time, as though seen by chance by a passing traveler on the way to some other place. The modernity of *House by the Railroad* lies in its power to convey the essence of America's rootless society. Hopper had found his personal vision, a dealer, and some recognition. From this time forward, little of significance changed in his art or in his life. He and Jo continued to live at 3 Washington Square North, leaving the city every summer, usually for the New England coast. Trips to New Mexico in 1925 and South Carolina in 1929 resulted in more watercolors with similar subject matter: architecture and landscape (see pages 41 and 50). From 1930 on, he and Jo spent most of their summers in South Truro on Cape Cod. Hopper's work after 1925 cannot easily be separated into periods or other more complex divisions based on style. Rather, by the mid-1920s, after he achieved his mature style, the formal elements of Hopper's vocabulary altered very little. Moreover, the subjects that Hopper explored were almost all variations on themes that had fascinated him before—as a child, a student, an illustrator, and a struggling artist.

THE MATURE WORK

Throughout his long career, as Hopper repeatedly shifted his approach in investigating certain subjects to reveal further meaning. Although Hopper did not offer political or social statements in his art, he was profoundly interested in mood and human interaction. Many have perceived a sense of loneliness, sometimes even of boredom, in much of Hopper's work. These psychological subtleties were probably intentional, although Hopper evaluated his achievements modestly:

> Just to paint a representation or design is not hard, but to express a thought in painting is. Thought is fluid. What you put on canvas is concrete, and it tends to direct the thought. The more you put on canvas the more you lose control of the thought. I've never been able to paint what I set out to paint.*

Hopper knew that any meaningful analysis of an artist's work must go beyond formal issues and consider content. Many have claimed that Hopper painted only what he observed, yet in his view « the great painters, with their intellect as master, have attempted to force this unwilling medium of paint and canvas into a record of their emotions.» ** For Hopper, painting was an intensely private experience which he saw primarily as a reflection of his own psyche: « So much of every art is an expression of the subconscious that it seems to me most of all the important qualities are put there unconsciously, and little of importance by the conscious intellect. But these are things for the psychologist to untangle.» *** And

---

* Quoted in Alexander Eliot, « Three Hundred Years of American Painting, » (New York: Time Inc., 1957), p. 298.
** Edward Hopper, « Notes on Painting, » in Alfred H. Barr, Jr., « Edward Hopper: Retrospective Exhibition » (New York: Museum of Modern Art, 1933), p. 17.
*** Edward Hopper to Charles H. Sawyer, letter of October 29, 1939. Quoted in full in Lloyd Goodrich, «Edward Hopper, » (New York: Harry N. Abrams, 1971), p. 164.

BAPTISTERY OF SAINT JOHN'S, 1929
Watercolor, 13⅝″ × 19⅝″ (35.2 × 50.5 cm)
Private collection

SOUTH TRURO CHURCH, 1930
Oil on canvas, 29″ × 43″ (73.7 × 109.3 cm)
Private collection

when asked what he was after in his 1963 painting *Sun in an Empty Room* (see page 87),
he replied: « I'm after ME. » *

When asked why he selected certain subjects over others, Hopper replied: « I do not exactly
know, unless it is that I believe them to be the best mediums for a synthesis of my inner
experience. » ** « Great art, » he wrote, « is the outward expression of an inner life in
the artist, and this inner life will result in his personal vision of the world. . . . The inner
life of a human being is a vast and varied realm. » *** Thus it is important to remember
that Hopper was directly concerned with emotional content in his art, even though he may
not have intended that content to be clearly interpretable. And while the meaning of
paintings may not always be accessible to us, Hopper's admitted search for personal
expression invites our investigation into the nature of the subjects he chose to paint. Hopper's
paintings, which seem to be ordinary scenes of everyday life, are in fact intensely personal,
often revealing several levels of meaning. He repeatedly infused commonplace subjects with
suggestions of eroticism, with solitary evocations of absence or aloneness, and, late in life,
with intimations of impeding loss, even death.

In interpreting Hopper's figural compositions it is essential to remember that Jo modeled
for all the women (see page 59). She also joined him in naming and fantasizing about the
characters in his paintings. Thus she played a crucial role in the rich drama of his
imagination, assisting him in transforming her image into one of his fantasy. A former
actress, Jo enabled Edward to function like the director giving a favorite actress many roles
to play. She also assisted him by shopping for the exact props he wanted to set up his pictures.
For example, Jo could appear young or old, seductive or disinterested. The eroticism of
Girlie Show (1941), a painting of a burlesque stripper with conical breasts and bright
red nipples who teases her audience by waving a blue garment she has already removed, is
both obvious and intentional (see page 76). The preparatory sketches reveal how Hopper
transformed Jo's petite form and aging features to that of the tall sultry redhead in the
painting (see pages 77 and 78). Hopper, who must have identified with the male figures
in the audience, shows this woman as desirable but untouchable, to be observed safely from
a distance. *Tables for Ladies* (1930) is somewhat more subtly suggestive (see page 44).
Viewed through a plate glass window, Hopper's central figure is a woman named Olga, who,
according to Jo's notes in the record books, was a « very blond, fine-looking waitress all in
white apron with bow in back. » With her cleavage slightly revealed, she is descendent of
the type of voluptuous woman who appears in paintings by Jan Steen and other seventeenth-
century Dutch artists. The title, *Tables for Ladies* is in itself suggestive: by depicting, in the
background, a gentleman dining with a properly dressed female companion whose back is
turned toward us, Hopper separates the blond Olga, a lusty and perhaps somewhat vulgar
woman, from the « ladies. » Olga's desirable body, her full breasts just visible, is suggestively
likened to the ripe fruit in the basket she reaches for and to the large grapefruits lined up
in the window. The association between female anatomy and fruit had been evoked in
literature since ancient times. Fruit, with its appeal to all the senses, is a natural symbol of
ripe human beauty. Hopper thought carefully about his props in this painting, and Jo reports

* O'Doherty, « Portrait: Edward Hopper, » p. 79.
** Goodrich, « Edward Hopper, » p. 152.
*** Edward Hopper, « Statements by Four Artists, » *Reality*, 1 (Spring 1953), p. 8.

CITY ROOFS, 1932. Oil on canvas, 29″ × 30″ (73.7 × 76.2 cm)
Private collection

Burly Cobb Hen Coop and Barn, 1930
Watercolor, 13½″ × 19½″ (34.3 × 49.5 cm)
Private collection

54

WHITE RIVER AT SHARON, 1937
Watercolor, 19⅜″ × 27½″ (49.2 × 69.8 cm)
The Sara Roby Foundation, New York

HOTEL ROOM, 1931 Oil on canvas, 60″ × 65″ (152.4 × 165.1 cm)
The Thyssen Bornemisza Collection, Lugano, Switzerland

having made extensive shopping trips to try to find the fruit and other items. Hopper's erotic imagery goes beyond fruit to include two raw chops—loins of meat—displayed prominently on a plate below Olga's hands. This meat also becomes associated with Olga, evoking the phrase to «lick one's chops,» meaning to await with pleasure or to relish. The erotic symbolism may reflect Hopper's familiarity with a Frans Hals painting at the Metropolitan Museum, *Merrymakers at Shrovetide*, in which the man at the right makes a suggestive gesture and the sausages and meats imply sexual appetite. Given Hopper's reluctance to reveal specific content in his work, *Tables for Ladies* is still unusually overt in its erotic suggestiveness. Hopper also portrayed woman as one half of a pair. His couples display a full range of emotions, from great passion, to disenchantment, to bitter disappointment. Works from Hopper's boyhood and young adulthood are usually much more optimistic. For example, with the romantic optimism of his youth still intact in the years just before he married, Hopper represented a couple passionately embracing in the etching *Les Deux Pigeons* (1920), with a waiter-voyeur observing them in a French outdoor café (see page 18).

When he wanted to convey disenchantment, Hopper turned to melancholy of dusk. In *Summer Twilight* (1920), he presented a man standing before a woman seated in a rocker, a sleeping dog lying by her side (see page 27). The man appears tense, his head angled downward, his hands in his jacket pockets, although the woman's fan implies that it is hot. She looks away, refusing to meet his gaze; a distance exists between them. The twilight of the title suggests not only the end of day and onset of night but, by allusion, the end of something, an impending termination, bringing with it uncertainty and gloom. With a pessimism that would later become characteristic of his work, Hopper captured a summer romance in its waning hours; the couple's idyllic summer setting will inevitably yield to the harsh realities of winter. Hopper's working sketches of *Cape Cod Evening* (1939) reveal that the painting evolved through several stages (see pages 72 and 73). Initially, he considered having only one figure: a woman seated on a doorstep with a dog standing close by, facing her. Then he tried the woman standing in blowing grass with the dog. His resolution—a man beckoning to the distracted dog from the doorstep with a morose-looking woman standing before the window—changed the entire content of the painting. We now confront a disenchanted couple: she detached, in a world of her own thoughts and dreams, he trying to communicate with the dog instead of with her. The evening here once again alludes to the twilight of a relationship. Communication does not work, and as Hopper commented on his inspiration and intention in *Cape Cod Evening*, even the dog listens only to a distant whippoorwill. The presence of a dog, both here and in the etching *Summer Twilight*, suggests that Hopper relied on this familiar symbol to make his own ironic comment on the couple's deteriorating relationship. Certainly, he knew and admired what he called «the honest simplicity of early Dutch and Flemish masters,»* embodied by Jan van Eyck's fifteenth-century *Arnolfini Marriage Portrait*, in which the dog is a symbol of fidelity and devotion. But Hopper may have also been aware that later, in Dutch paintings of the seventeenth century, a dog often connoted lasciviousness or gluttony, in an ironical reversal of the original symbolism.

In Hopper's 1947 painting *Summer Evening*, the time of day again corresponds to a stage in a couple's relationship (see page 75). The young couple in the painting—she scantily clad

* Hopper, « John Sloan, » p. 173.

for the summer's heat—seem engrossed in an unpleasant discussion while they lean against the wall of a porch with only the overly bright electric light—no romantic moonlight for them. The porch of the clapboard house recalls Hopper's boyhood home in Nyack, suggesting that his conception in *Summer Evening* was based on distant memories. Indeed, he claimed that the painting had been in the back of his head «for twenty years.»* The woman's face is twisted in a grimace, while her shoulders are arched defensively—like the back of a provoked cat. The man, the focus of her discontent, holds his left hand on his chest as if protesting. Hopper poignantly expressed the torment of a passion gone sour: the fresh excitement of spring about to turn into the disillusion of autumn. As in *Summer Twilight* and *Cape Cod Evening*, dusk here symbolizes the melancholy of lost desire, opportunity surrendering to inevitable decay.

The link between twilight and lost desire is a recurring theme in French Symbolist poetry which Hopper first came to know as a student under Robert Henri. As Hopper's own pessimism developed, *his* evening came to signify despair—a sense of loss at what might have been. The alienated characters of *Soir Bleu* seem to embody Symbolist poems: Rimbaud's «Sensation» begins «Par les soirs bleus d'été» («In the blue summer evenings»). Hopper has captured the mood of the poem—even to the silent people staring—as if frozen in a trance, with blank minds: «Je ne parlerai pas, je ne penserai rien...» («I will not speak, I will have no thoughts»).** Hopper's vision of Paris as a decadent city was underlined and colored by the images of the Symbolist poets. Hopper's love of Symbolist poetry persisted throughout his life; as late as 1951 he gave his wife a volume of Rimbaud's poetry for Christmas, complete with his own inscription to her, in French: «A la petite chatte qui découvre ses griffes presque tous les jours. Joyeux Noël.» («To the little cat who bares her claws almost every day. Merry Christmas.») It is the melancholy spirit of Symbolist poetry, which so appealed to Hopper, that pervades *Room in New York* and its successors: all are poignant comments on the fragility of erotic relationship (see page 61). The enduring frustration of eros gone stale is a much repeated theme in Hopper's maturity. His friend and fellow painter Charles Burchfield observed: «The element of silence that seems to pervade every one of his [Hopper's] major works... can almost be deadly, as in *Room in New York*....»*** The silence of Hopper's couples, together with their postures and expressions, announces an erotic despair, a complete failure to communicate. How poignant that Burchfield remarked on the almost deadly *silence* in a picture where a woman has her finger poised on a piano key, about to strike a note. The piano serves as a reminder of the absence of spoken communication. In this encounter playing the piano offers the woman an all too necessary diversion, for her companion, lost in his newspaper, appears to desire solitude—escape from her. As he ignores her, she seems resigned and melancholy.

Hopper's *Room in New York* sets up a pronounced, if stereotyped, male-female dichotomy: he sits on the left reading a newspaper, emphasizing his intellect and pragmatic character while she, seated opposite him, turns to make music, revealing her artistic, more emotional

---

* «Traveling Man,» *Time*, January 19, 1948, p. 60.
** See «Rimbaud Complete Works, Selected Letters,» Translation, introduction and notes by Wallace Fowlie (Chicago: University of Chicago Press, 1966), p. 17.
*** Charles Burchfield, «Hopper: Career of Silent Poetry,» *Art News*, 49 March 1950, p. 17.

Jo Seated, 1925. Conté on paper, 22" × 15" (56 × 38 cm)
Whitney Museum of American Art, New York. Bequest of Josephine N. Hopper

nature. She is shown about to disturb the deadly silence, interjecting her presence, demanding his attention. He is introspective, withdrawn, unresponsive. The composition of *Room in New York* is significant in that it links Hopper's mature work to his earlier production as an illustrator. The germ of *Room in New York* can be found in one of Hopper's illustrations for Carroll D. Murphy's «What Makes Men Buy?» published in «System, the Magazine of Business» (a forerunner to «Business Week») in September 1912 (see page 16). In this illustration, we find the prototype of the tuned-out male, the man lost in his newspaper, ignoring his female companion. The composition is skillfully organized by the rectangular shapes of architecture, echoed by the framed picture hanging on the wall behind the couple, a device Hopper probably encountered in the work of Edgar Degas. Twenty years later, in painting *Room in New York*, Hopper again utilized the rectangles of architecture to articulate an interior space, but he dramatically separated the viewer from the interior through a window ledge that extends across the canvas. He repeated the centrally placed round table, but shifted the woman from behind it to its side, directly across from the man, thereby achieving a more intense feeling of alienation. The painting also reminds us of Hopper's love of movies, for its composition seems especially cinematic — like a close-up shot, a camera penetrating beyond a building's exterior walls to reveal a drama already in progress.

Reluctant as always to comment on his painting's content, Hopper nonetheless admitted that he had not simply painted an observed scene in *Room in New York*:

> The idea had been in my mind a long time before I painted it. It was suggested by glimpses of lighted interiors seen as I walked along city streets at night, probably near the district where I live (Washington Square) although it's no particular street or house, but is really a synthesis of many impressions. *

Just as Hopper linked erotic disenchantment to the melancholy of dusk, he associated erotic anxiety with night. This mood can be found in works ranging from his 1918 etching *Night on the El Train* to his later oil paintings *Night Windows*, *Office at Night*, and *Nighthawks*. The man and woman riding alone in *Night on the El Train* turn intensely toward each other, engaged, even provoked, by the other's presence (see page 26). In *Office at Night* such an intimate confrontation is only suggested (see pages 88 and 89). An erotic encounter between a man and his curvaceous secretary is alluded to by the woman's posture and seductive dress (including high-heeled pumps and, as Jo noted in the record book, «plenty of lipstick») as well as by the breeze blowing on the window shade. In their notations in the record book, the Hoppers identified the woman as «Shirley» and captioned the work «Confidentially Yours. Room 1005» revealing the potential eroticism they perceived in the encounter. Hopper's intention to create a sultry female character can be seen in the evolution from his preparatory sketches to the final painting. In the early sketches, based on Jo, the figure of the secretary is plain, even dowdy; in the end she is transformed into an alluring, coquettish creature. Psychic and sexual tension is implied not only by her body language and dress but by the perspectival line of recession that aligns her with the

* Quoted in « Such a Life, » *Life*, 102 (August 1935), p. 48.

ROOM IN NEW YORK, 1932. Oil on canvas, 29″ × 36″ (73.7 × 91.5 cm)
Sheldon Memorial Art Gallery, University of Nebraska, Lincoln. F. M. Hall Collection

DAWN IN PENNSYLVANIA, 1942
Oil on canvas, 24½″ × 44½″ (62.3 × 113 cm)
Private collection

SHAKESPEARE AT DUSK, 1935
Oil on canvas, 17″ × 25″ (43.2 × 63.5 cm)
Collection: Mr. and Mrs. Carl Lobell

63

THE CIRCLE THEATRE, 1936
Oil on canvas, 27″ × 36″ (68.5 × 91.5 cm)
Private collection

65

man. The open door, file drawer, and window allude to her openess, to the possibility of an erotic encounter. Hopper's inspiration to depict an office scene, a subject rarely portrayed in art, comes not only from his experiences illustrating offices for « System » and other magazines but also from such paintings as *The Cotton Exchange, New Orleans* and *Sulking,* both by Edgar Degas, one of the artists Hopper admired most. The furnishings of the office depicted in Hopper's 1940 canvas date back to the 1910s, when he produced his office illustrations.

A confluence of several meanings is common to Hopper's paintings. Three of his most significant themes — eros, solitude, and death — are combined in his masterpiece *Nighthawks* (see page 81). Hopper, as we have seen, associated eros with night. The man and woman almost touching hands in the uneasy atmosphere of *Nighthawks* are juxtaposed against the solitary diner seated across the counter, suggesting that only eros can assuage the loneliness of night. Critical assessments of this work have focused on its sinister qualities, which have been compared to Van Gogh's *Night Café* a painting that probably inspired Hopper. One writer even perceived in *Nighthawks* a mood of impending violence: « In these predatory times it would not be surprising to see one of the three draw a gun and demand the contents of the cash register. » [*] *Nighthawks* may also have been inspired by Hopper's admiration for Ernest Hemingway's short story « The Killers, » which he admired so much that he wrote a fan letter on it to « Scribner's Magazine » when it was published in 1927. There is something in both the setting and mood of *Nighthawks* that evokes « The Killers. » Hemingway's tale is set in the evening in a lunchroom:

> Outside it was getting dark. The street-light came on outside the window. The two men at the counter read the menu. From the other side of the counter Nick Adams watched them. He had been talking to George when they came in. [**]

Hopper has placed the same number of characters around his counter; his couple corresponds to the two men in the Hemingway story who « sat leaning forward, their elbows on the counter. » What Hopper must have appreciated most in the Hemingway story — the suspense of impending violence that never takes place — is suggested in *Nighthawks.* Even his choice of a title relates to « The Killers, » for hawk is a slang term for a person who preys on others as well as a verb meaning « to hunt on the wing. » In the record book, Jo referred to the woman's companion as a « nighthawk (beak). » Using « nighthawks, » however, to refer to people who are just habitually up or moving about late at night seems excessive when the more innocuous « nightowls » might serve that purpose. « Nighthawks » suggest predatory activity. Perhaps the cash register, the only object visible across the street through an illuminated store window, hints of the greed of these sinister nocturnal prowlers. In the days of mobsters and armed robberies, the register was often the very object of hunters in the night, the focus of their evil intentions. Yet the setting of *Nighthawks* also betrays a certain innocence, recalling scenes among Hopper's illustrations of the 1910s (see page 16). The poignancy of this painting derives from its dramatic spatial configuration and

[*] Loring Holmes Dodd, « Hopper Show Proves Him Stark Realist, » *Worcester Evening Gazette,* May 31, 1950.
[**] Ernest Hemingway, « The Killers, » reprinted in « The Short Stories of Ernest Hemingway » (New York: Modern Library, 1938), p. 377.

Study for « New York Movie », 1939. Conté on paper, 15″ × 11¹/₁₆″ (38 × 28 cm)
Whitney Museum of American Art, New York. Bequest of Josephine N. Hopper

FRENCH SIX-DAY BICYCLE RIDER, 1937
Oil on canvas, 17″ × 19″ (43.2 × 48.2 cm)
Collection: Mr. and Mrs. Albert Hackett

evocative lighting, which create an atmosphere conveying the vulnerability of anyone out in the disquieting night.

When Hopper turned to the theme of solitude, he found metaphors in compositions devoid of human presence, particularly in locations where people might be expected: the street in *Early Sunday Morning*, the mall in Central Park in *Shakespeare at Dusk*, and the interior in *Sun in an Empty Room* (see pages 43, 63, and 87). Hopper revealed himself most openly by titling a painting of a deserted house and road *Solitude* (see page 85) in which he depicted a Cape Cod vista in autumn when the deep grass turns a golden tone. Hopper liked to remain on the Cape through October, after the summertime crowds departed. It was because Cape Cod remained warmer longer than Maine or Cape Ann that Hopper preferred to spend his summers there. When one interviewer commented on the lack of communication in his paintings and on the «profound loneliness,» Hopper replied: «It's probably a reflection of my own, if I may say, loneliness. I don't know. It could be the whole human condition.»* Solitude as a recurring theme in Hopper's œuvre is often expressed through the portrayal of a lone figure in situations where other artists would depict crowds. Such figures include the usherette in *New York Movie* (see page 65), and the man in a deserted urban setting in *Night Shadows* and *Sunday* (see pages 80 and 42). The desire for solitude often necessitates escape from the company of others. Many motifs alluding to escape recur in Hopper's work: windows, railroad stations, trains, tracks, highways, boats at sea, reading, the theater, and the movies. Boats at sea appear to be the ideal realization of escape in *Monhegan Boat*, *The Lee Shore*, and *The Martha McKean of Wellfleet* (see pages 25, 82, and 83). Although the vessels often appear to have been forever frozen in motion, they convey the solitary romance of the seafarer which caught Hopper's imagination.

Every summer Hopper and Jo escaped New York's heat and crowds and took refuge in rural New England. In 1934, after spending four summers in South Truro, Massachusetts, Hopper and his wife decided to build a simple home there with a studio space to enable them to paint outdoors. Before this they had stayed in a small rented house on the farm of A. B. Cobb, (see page 54), which they called «Bird Cage Cottage» because it let in rain, wind, and animals with equal freedom. Over the years on the Cape, Hopper painted the simple buildings, roads, and natural forms of the landscape. Focusing on the effect of intense sunlight in *South Truro Church* (1930) or the somber tones and softer light of autumn in *October on Cape Cod* (1946), he conveyed the drama of the forms he observed and saved them from banality (see pages 51 and 84). According to Jo's description of *Cape Cod Morning* (1950) in the record book, Hopper had been painting fields in September with a «blondish housewife (appraising early A. M. weather) in pink cotton dress.» She noted that the «painting went off speedily, no interrupting from sketches in Orleans.» She claimed: «It's a woman looking out to see if the weather's good enough to hang out her wash,» prompting Hopper to rejoin: «Did I say that? You're making it Norman Rockwell. From my point of view she's just looking out the window, just looking out the window.»** *Cape Cod Morning*, like other paintings of women in interiors, relates to Hopper's interest in sunlight and to the placement of a woman by a window as seen in Dutch paintings by Vermeer, de Hoogh, and others (see page 74).

* Edward Hopper, interview with Aline Saarinen, «Sunday Show,» NBC-TV, 1964, transcript, p. 3.
** Jo and Edward Hopper, quoted in «Gold for Gold,» *Time*, May 30, 1955, p. 72.

GAS, 1940
Oil on canvas, 26¼″ × 40¼″ (66.7 × 102.2 cm)
The Museum of Modern Art, New York
Mrs. Simon Guggenheim Fund

FOUR LANE ROAD, 1956
Oil on canvas, 27½″ × 41½″ (70 × 105.5 cm)
Private collection

71

Study for « Cape Cod Evening », 1939
Conté, charcoal, and pencil on paper, 15" × 22⅛" (38 × 56.2 cm)
Whitney Museum of American Art, New York. Bequest of Josephine N. Hopper

Drawing for « Cape Cod Evening », 1939
Conté, charcoal, and pencil on paper
8½" × 11" (21.5 × 28 cm)
Whitney Museum of American Art
New York
Bequest of Josephine N. Hopper

72

CAPE COD EVENING, 1939
Oil on canvas, 30¼″ × 40¼″ (76.8 × 102.2 cm)
National Gallery of Art, Washington D.C. John Hay Whitney Collection

CAPE COD MORNING, 1950
Oil on canvas, 34″ × 40″ (86.3 × 101.5 cm)
The Sara Roby Foundation, New York

SUMMER EVENING, 1947
Oil on color, 30″ × 42″ (76.2 × 106.8 cm)
Collection: Mr. and Mrs. Gilbert H. Kinney

GIRLIE SHOW, 1941
Oil on canvas
32″ × 38″ (81.3 × 96.5 cm)
Private collection

▷
Interior of Burlesque Theatre, Times Square, 1941
Charcoal and stump on paper
11⅞″ × 8⅞″ (30.2 × 22.5 cm)
Corcoran Gallery of Art, Washington D.C.

76

Sketch for « Girlie Show », 1941
Conté on paper, 13¼" × 15" (33.7 × 38 cm)
Whitney Museum of American Art, New York. Bequest of Josephine N. Hopper

When Hopper grew restless or found himself unable to paint, he sometimes traveled with Jo. They visited Mexico several times and traveled extensively about the United States, visiting particularly New England, the South, and the Far West. Along the way, Hopper became fascinated with the psychology and environment of travelers—hotels, trains, highways, and gas stations. Works like *Gas* and *Dawn in Pennsylvania* convey a sense of eerie expectation as well as the loneliness of the traveler, removed from the comforts of a familiar environment (see pages 70 and 62).

Hotel Room powerfully expresses Hopper's interest in solitude (see page 56). In this painting of ambitious scale, a masterful geometric simplicity achieves monumentality. The spare vertical and diagonal bands of color and sharp electric shadows present a concise and intense drama in the night. The tall, slender, pensive woman sits on a bed, her head cast downward as she considers a piece of yellow paper in her hand. According to Jo's record, the paper is a timetable that the woman has just consulted. Whatever she has learned seems to have upset her, as the clothing strewn about the room suggests. Combining poignant subject matter with such a powerful formal arrangement, Hopper produced a composition of strength and refinement—simple enough to appeal to an abstract sensibility—yet layered with meaning for the sensitive observer. This was the first of several paintings Hopper set in hotel bedrooms and lobbies, all suggesting the disorienting experience of life away from home. «To me the most important thing is the sense of going on. You know how beautiful things are when you're traveling.» * In recording local color, Hopper captured a sense of place with a notably individual vision. His trip to Santa Fe, New Mexico, in the summer of 1925 was characteristic. He found it difficult to work with such picturesque beauty and intensity of light. At first he painted a train there, but eventually he made watercolors of local sights such as *Adobe Houses* (see page 41). Another trip—to South Royalton, Vermont, in September 1937—produced several watercolors of the local landscape, including the half-dead tree and a railroad embankment depicted in *White River at Sharon* (see page 55).

Hopper chose his subjects for their fascinating forms or content rather than for their beauty. He was naturally attracted to architecture and painted both interior and exterior views of buildings. He often focused on specific architectural details, such as stairways and rooftops, which attracted him wherever he was—from New York to Paris or Mexico (see page 53). In *Two Puritans* Hopper's composition seems strangely animated, as if the two houses had personalities (see page 86). The windows, shutters, and doors suggest facial features, recalling the work of Hopper's friend Charles Burchfield. Like the deserted depictions of architecture, Hopper's repeated travel motifs, usually seen empty, express the desire to escape—the quest for solitude. The theme of the road and the railroads spans his entire career, from his boyhood to his penultimate painting, *Chair Car* (see page 91). In his later years, pessimistic by his own admission, Hopper began to focus more and more on death—the ultimate escape, an eternal solitude. As his concern with death deepened in his old age, Hopper made it the theme of some of his last paintings.

At age eighty-three Hopper painted *Two Comedians*, which he intended as a personal statement, a farewell of sorts. As Jo later confirmed, the painting represented the two of

* Quoted in William C. Seitz, « Edward Hopper in São Paulo 9 » (Washington, D. C.: Smithsonian Press, 1969), p. 22.

them gracefully bowing out (see page 90). Both were in their eighties and had been ill; Hopper would die less than two years later and Jo the following year. In contrast to his repeated depictions of noncommunicative couples, as in *Room in New York* and *Cape Cod Evening*, here the tall male comedian, representing Hopper, takes the hand of the diminutive comedian, representing Jo. They are like the young lovers Pierrot and Pierrette from the commedia dell'arte. In death, it appears, Hopper preferred company, wanting Jo by his side. She described *Two Comedians* as «a dark stage (and what a stage, strong as the deck of a ship) and two small figures out of a pantomime. *Poignant.*»* By his choice of theme, Hopper suggested his acceptance of life's ironies—his realization of the folly of human existence.

Hopper once remarked of artists in general: «Ninety percent of them are forgotten ten minutes after they're dead.» His cynicism certainly did not accurately predict his own enduring and growing reputation. Yet he also knew what was memorable: «The only quality that endures in art is a personal vision of the world. Methods are transient: personality is enduring.»** Hopper's œuvre demonstrates the uniqueness of his vision, making his images as relevant today as the day he created them. His art speaks not to one country or to one time but to all who grapple with the trials of civilization as they occur in daily life.

* Jo Hopper to Margaret McKellar, letter of November 14, 1965.
** Edward Hopper, «A Statement by the Chairman of the Jury,» *Twenty-Second Biennial Exhibition of Contemporary American Oil Paintings* (Washington, D.C.: Corcoran Gallery of Art, 1951), p. 7.

Night Shadows, 1921
Etching, 7" × 8⅜"
(17.8 × 21.3 cm)
The Metropolitan Museum
of Art, New York
Harris Brisbane Dick Fund

NIGHTHAWKS, 1942. Oil on canvas, 33¼″ × 60⅛″ (85 × 152.7 cm)
The Art Institute of Chicago, Friends of American Art

THE LEE SHORE, 1941
Oil on canvas, 28¼" × 43" (71.7 × 109.2 cm)
Private collection

82

THE MARTHA McKEAN OF WELLFLEET, 1944
Oil on canvas, 32″ × 50″ (81.3 × 127 cm)
The Thyssen Bornemisza Collection, Lugano, Switzerland

OCTOBER ON CAPE COD, 1946
Oil on canvas, 26″ × 42″ (66 × 106.8 cm)
Collection: Loretta and Robert K. Lifton, New York

Two Puritans, 1945
Oil on canvas, 30″ × 40″ (76.2 × 101.5 cm)
Private collection

Sun in an Empty Room, 1963
Oil on canvas, 28¾" × 39½" (73 × 100.5 cm)
Private collection

OFFICE AT NIGHT, 1940
Oil on canvas, 22⅛" × 25" (56.2 × 63.5 cm)
Walker Art Center Minneapolis
Gift of the T. B. Walker Foundation

Drawing for Office at Night, 1940
Conté and charcoal with touches of white, 15" × 19⅝" (38 × 50 cm)
Whitney Museum of American Art, New York
Bequest of Josephine N. Hopper

Two Comedians, 1965
Oil on canvas, 29″ × 40″ (73.5 × 101.5 cm)
Collection: Mr. and Mrs. Frank Sinatra

BIOGRAPHY

1882 July 22, Edward Hopper born in Nyack, New York, son of Garret Henry Hopper and Elizabeth Griffiths Smith Hopper.

1888–99 Attended local private school; graduated from Nyack High School. As a teenager, built himself a catboat with wood provided by his father.

1899–1900 Studied illustration at the Correspondence School of Illustrating, a commercial art school at 114 West Thirty-fourth Street in New York City.

1900–06 Studied illustration at the New York School of Art with Arthur Keller and Frank Vincent DuMond, then painting under Robert Henri, William Merritt Chase, and Kenneth Hayes Miller.

1906 Employed as an illustrator by C. C. Phillips & Company, 24 East Twenty-second Street, New York. October. Lived at 48 Rue de Lille in Paris, in a building owned by the Eglise Evangélique Baptiste. Continued friendship with Patrick Henry Bruce.

1907 June 27, left Paris to travel to London, where he visited the National Gallery, the Wallace Collection, and Westminster Abbey.
July 19, left London for Holland. Visited Amsterdam and Haarlem, where Robert Henri was conducting a summer school for American students.
Arrived in Berlin on July 26.
August 1, arrived in Brussels for two days before returning to Paris.
August 21, sailed for New York.
Worked as a commercial artist in New York.

1909 March 18, arrived in Paris via Cherbourg.
May, painted outdoors along the Seine frequently. Visited Fontainebleau.
June, visited Saint-Germain-en-Laye.
July 31, sailed on Holland-America Line to New York, arriving on August 9.

1910 May, returned to Paris. May 26, left Paris for Madrid. While in Spain, visited Toledo and attended a bullfight. Returned to Paris on June 11. July 1, sailed for New York.
Set up studio at 53 East Fifty-ninth Street in New York. Began to earn his living by commercial art and illustration; painted in free time and in the summers.

1912 Summer in Gloucester, Massachusetts, where he painted with Leon Kroll.

1913 Death of father.
February 15 to March 15, exhibited one oil in the New York Armory Show, which sold for $250, his first sale of a painting.
December, moved to 3 Washington Square North, New York, where he lived until his death.

1914 Summer in Ogunquit, Maine.

1915 Took up etching. Second summer in Ogunquit, Maine.

1916–19 Summers on Monhegan Island, Maine.

1918 October, Hopper's poster Smash the Hun won the first prize in the « citizen's class » nationwide competition of the National Service Section of the United States Shipboard Emergency Fleet Corporation.

1923 Attended the Whitney Studio Club evening sketch class and made numerous life drawings.
Summer in Gloucester, Massachusetts. Produced the last of his etchings. Began to paint watercolors regularly.

December 7, sold The Mansard Roof to the Brooklyn Museum for $100.

1924 Married Josephine Verstille Nivison on July 9 at the Eglise Evangélique on West Sixteenth Street, New York. Guy Pène du Bois was best man. Summer in Gloucester, Massachusetts.

1925 June through late September, visited James Mountain, Colorado, and Santa Fe, New Mexico.

1926 Took train trip to Eastport, Maine, for seven weeks, then on to Gloucester, Massachusetts.

1927 Bought an automobile.
Summer at Two Lights, Cape Elizabeth, Maine. Visited Mrs. Summer at Two Lights. Visited Mrs. Catherine Budd in Charlestown, New Hampshire, on return trip. Made an excursion across the Connecticut River into Vermont.

1928 January 20, made his last print, a drypoint, Portrait of Jo.
Summer in Gloucester, Massachusetts. Trip to Ogunquit, Maine, to visit Annette and Clarence K. Chatterton of Vassar. Traveled through New Hampshire and Vermont before returning to New York.

1929 April 1 to May 11, trip to Charleston, South Carolina.
Summer, visit to Topsfield, Massachusetts, home of Mr. and Mrs. Samuel A. Tucker. Second stay at Two Lights, Cape Elizabeth, Maine. Trips to Essex and Pemaquid Point.

1930 Visited with Grace and Edward Root at Hampton College, Clinton, New York, before going to South Truro, Massachusetts, on Cape Cod. Rented A. B. Cobb's house, « Bird Cage Cottage, » on a hill.

1931–32 Summers in « Bird Cage Cottage » in South Truro, Massachusetts.

1932 March, elected an associate member of the National Academy of Design, a nomination he declined because the Academy had rejected his paintings in years past. Took additional studio space at 3 Washington Square North, New York.

1933 Visited Murray Bay in Quebec Province, Canada, then went on to Ogunquit and Two Lights, Maine, and Boston. Returned to South Truro, Massachusetts, to « Bird Cage Cottage. » October 1, purchased land in South Truro and returned to New York later that month.

1934 Early May, went to South Truro, Massachusetts. Stayed at the Jenness house while building a studio house at South Truro (in which he and Jo stayed through late November and spent almost every successive summer).

1935 March, death of mother.
Trip from South Truro to East Montpelier, Vermont.

1936 Visited Plainfield, Vermont.

1937 September, visited South Royalton (White River Valley), Vermont.

1938 September, visited South Royalton during hurricane. Stayed in South Truro, Massachusetts, through late November.
Acquired rear studio at 3 Washington Square North for Jo.

1939 Returned to New York early from summer at South Truro in order to travel to Pittsburgh, Pennsylvania, to be on the jury of the Carnegie Institute.
Painted no watercolors this year or next, but painted oils in South Truro studio.

1940 Traveled from South Truro to New York to register

to vote. Returned to New York early from the Cape in order to vote for Wendell Willkie over Franklin Roosevelt.

1941 Spring, trip to Albany to jury exhibition.
Summer (May through July), traveled to Colorado and Utah. Drove through Nevada desert to Pacific Coast and north through California to Oregon. Returned via Wyoming and Yellowstone Park. Returned to house at South Truro late in August.

1943 March, traveled to Washington to be on the Corcoran jury.
Summer, made first trip to Mexico, by train. Visited Mexico City, Saltillo, and Monterrey, returning in early October. Painted four watercolors from roof of Guarhado House, Saltillo, and two from window of Monterrey Hotel.

1944 Summer in South Truro. Trip to Boston and Hyannis for automobile repairs.

1945 May, elected member of the National Institute of Arts and Letters.

1946 May, drove to Saltillo, Mexico, and painted four watercolors. July in Grand Tetons; August through November in South Truro.

1947 November, trip to Indianapolis to serve on jury of exhibition of Indiana artists.

1951 May 28, left by car for third trip to Mexico via Chattanooga, Tennessee. In Saltillo for a month. Visited Santa Fe, New Mexico, briefly on returning. Stayed in South Truro until November.

1952 Chosen by the American Federation of Arts as one of the four artists to represent the United States in the Venice Biennale.
Summer in South Truro.
December, left for Mexico. Stayed eight days in El Paso, Texas. Visited Posada de la Presa Guanajuato and spent one month at Mitla, Oaxaca. Visited Puebla and returned via Laredo.

1953 March 1, returned to New York from Mexico, where he painted two watercolors.
Joined Raphael Soyer and other representational painters as a member of the editorial committee of *Reality*.
Summer in South Truro. September 15, visited Gloucester and went to Charlestown, New Hampshire, to visit Mrs. William Proctor.

1955 March 31, to May 1, visited Mexico. Summer and fall in South Truro.

1956 Awarded Huntington Hartford Foundation fellowship. December 9, arrived at Huntington Hartford Foundation, Pacific Palisades, California.

1957 June 6, left Huntington Hartford Foundation. July 22 through late October, in South Truro.

1959 July 15, to South Truro for summer.
October trip to Manchester, New Hampshire, for November one-man exhibition at Currier Gallery of Art.
December, Currier exhibition shown at Rhode Island School of Design. Visited Providence, Rhode Island, as the guest of Mr. and Mrs. Malcolm Chace.

1960 Spring, met with the artists' group who had published *Reality* at home of John Koch to protest the predominance of the « gobbledegook influences » of abstract art at the Whitney Museum and the Museum of Modern Art in New York.

1964 May, unable to paint because of illness.

1965 July 16, death of Hopper's sister, Marion, in Nyack, New York.
Finished last painting, *Two Comedians*.

1967 May 15, died in his studio at 3 Washington Square North.

PRINCIPAL EXHIBITIONS

1908 March 9–31, included in « Exhibition of Paintings and Drawings by Contemporary American Artists » at 43–45 West Forty-second Street; showed for the first time with several other former students of Robert Henri.

1913 February 15–March 15, included in the New York Armory Show (International Exhibition of Modern Art).

1920 January 14–28, first one-man show. Whitney Studio Club, 147 West Fourth Street.

1924 October–November, Frank K. M. Rehn Gallery, exhibition of recent watercolors.

1933 November 1–December 7, retrospective at the Museum of Modern Art. Traveled to the Arts Club of Chicago.

1950 February 11–March 26, retrospective at Whitney Museum of American Art. Traveled to the Museum of Fine Arts, Boston, and the Detroit Institute of Arts.

1952 One of four artists chosen by the American Federation of Arts to represent the United States in the Venice Biennale.

1962 October–November, « The Complete Graphic York of Edward Hopper, » Philadelphia Museum of Art; included fifty-two prints. Exhibit traveled to Worcester Art Museum.

1964 September 29–November 29, retrospective at the Whitney Museum of American Art. Exhibit traveled to the Art Institute of Chicago.

1967 September 22–January 8, 1968, featured in the United States Exhibition at the Bienal de São Paulo 9, Brazil.

1979 September 27–December 9, « Edward Hopper: Prints and Illustrations, » at the Whitney Museum of American Art. Included the complete prints and a selection of illustrations shown for the first time. Exhibit traveled to Museum of Fine Arts, Boston; Georgia Museum of Art, Athens; Detroit Institute of Arts; Fort Worth Art Museum; Milwaukee Art Center.

1980 September 23–January 18, 1981, « Edward Hopper: The Art and the Artist, » at the Whitney Museum of American Art. Exhibit traveled to the Hayward Gallery, London; Stedelijk Museum, Amsterdam; Städtische Kunstalle, Düsseldorf; The Art Institute of Chicago; San Francisco Museum of Modern Art.
October 16–November 30, « Edward Hopper: The Formative Years, » San José Museum of Art, California. Exhibit traveled to Newport Museum and Art Gallery, Wales; Fruit Market Gallery, Edinburgh; Westfälisches Landesmuseum für Kunst und Kulturgeschichte, Münster; Mostyn Gallery, Llandudo, Wales; Padiglione d'Arte Contemporanea, Milan.

1982 March 5–April 4, « The World of Edward Hopper, » Art Gallery of South Australia, Adelaide; National Gallery of Victoria, Melbourne; Queensland Art Gallery, Brisbane; Art Gallery of New South Wales, Sydney.

SELECTED BIBLIOGRAPHY

BARKER, Virgil. « The Etchings of Edward Hopper, » *The Arts*, 5 (June 1924), pp. 323–25.

BARR, Alfred H., Jr. *Edward Hopper: Retrospective Exhibition.* New York: Museum of Modern Art, 1933.

BURCHFIELD, Charles. « Hopper: Career of Silent Poetry, » *Art News*, 49 (March 1950), pp. 14–17.

BURREY, Suzanne. « Edward Hopper: The Emptying Spaces, » *Arts Digest*, April 1, 1955, pp. 8–10.

DU BOIS, Guy Pène. « Edward Hopper, Draughtsman, » *Shadowland*, 7 (October 1922), pp. 22–23.

——. « The American Paintings of Edward Hopper, » *Creative Art*, 8 (March 1931), pp. 187–91.

——. *Artists Say the Silliest Things.* New York: American Artists Group and Duell, Sloan, and Pearce, 1940.

GOODRICH, Lloyd. « The Paintings of Edward Hopper, » *The Arts*, 2 (March 1927), pp. 134–38.

——. *Edward Hopper: Retrospective Exhibition.* New York: Whitney Museum of American Art, 1950.

——. *Edward Hopper: Exhibition and Catalogue.* New York: Whitney Museum of American Art, 1964.

——. *Edward Hopper.* New York: Harry N. Abrams, 1971.

——. *Edward Hopper: Selections from the Hopper Bequest to the Whitney Museum of American Art.* New York: Whitney Museum of American Art, 1971.

HOPPER, Edward « Books » (review of Malcolm C. Salaman, *Fine Prints of the Year*, 1925), *The Arts*, 9 (March 1926), pp. 172–74.

——. « John Sloan and the Philadelphians, » *The Arts*, 11 (April 1927), pp. 168–78.

——. « Books » (review of Vernon Blake, *The Art and Craft of Drawing*), *The Arts*, 11 (June 1927), pp. 333–34.

——. « Charles Burchfield: American, » *The Arts*, 14 (July 1928), pp. 5–12.

——. « Edward Hopper Objects » (letter to Nathaniel Poussette-Dart). *The Art of Today*, 6 (February 1935), p. 11.

——. « Statements by Four Artists, » *Reality*, 1 (Spring 1953), p. 8.

KENT, Rockwell. *It's Me O Lord: The Autobiography of Rockwell Kent.* New York: Dodd, Mead, 1955.

KUH, Katharine. *The Artist's Voice. Talks with Seventeen Artists.* New York: Harper & Row, 1962.

LANES, Jerrold. « Edward Hopper: French Formalist, Ash Can Realist, Neither or Both, » *Artforum*, 7 (October 1968), pp. 44–50.

LEVIN, Gail. *Edward Hopper at Kennedy Galleries.* New York: Kennedy Galleries, 1977.

——. « Edward Hopper's "Office at Night," » *Arts Magazine*, 52 (January 1978), pp. 134–47.

——. « Edward Hopper, Francophile, » *Arts Magazine*, 53 (June 1979), pp. 114–21.

——. *Edward Hopper as Illustrator.* New York: W. W. Norton, in association with the Whitney Museum of American Art, 1979.

——. « Edward Hopper as Printmaker and Illustrator: Some Correspondences, » *The Print Collector's Newsletter*, 10 (September-October 1979), pp. 121–23.

——. *Edward Hopper: The Complete Prints.* New York: W. W. Norton in association with the Whitney Museum of American Art, 1979.

——. « Some of the Finest Examples of American Printmaking, » *Art News*, 78 (September 1979), pp. 90–93.

——. *Edward Hopper: The Art and the Artist.* New York: W. W. Norton in association with the Whitney Museum of American Art, 1980. London: W. W. Norton, 1981. Munich: Schirmer/Mosel Verlag GmbH, 1981.

——. « Edward Hopper als Radierer, » *Die Kunstzeitschift*, (April 1980), pp. 38–49.

——. « Josephine Verstille Nivison Hopper, » *Woman's Art Journal*, 1 (Spring-Summer 1980), pp. 28–32.

——. « Edward Hopper and the Whitney, » *Horizon*, 23 (September 1980), pp. 52–53.

——. « Edward Hopper's Evening, » *The Connoisseur*, 205 (September 1980), pp. 56–63.

——. « Edward Hopper: The Artist, » *Museum Magazine*, 1 (September-October 1980), pp. 66–67.

——. « Edward Hopper's Process of Self-Analysis, » *Art News*, 79 (October 1980), pp. 144–47.

——. « Edward Hopper: The Influence of Theater and Film, » *Arts Magazine*, 55 (October 1980), pp. 123–27.

——. « Hopper, un gigante del realismo americano: l'America è sola al mondo, » *Bolaffi Arte*, 7 (October 1980), pp. 42–48.

——. *Edward Hopper: Gli anni della formazione*, Milan: Electa Editrice, 1981.

——. *Edward Hopper: Das Frühwerk.* Münster: Westfälisches Landesmuseum für Kunst und Kulturgeschichte, April 1981.

——. « Edward Hopper's "Nighthawks," » *Arts Magazine*, 55 (May 1981), pp. 154–161.

——. « Editor's Statement, » Edward Hopper Symposium at the Whitney Museum of American Art, *Art Journal*, 41 (Summer 1981), special Hopper issue includes articles by Linda Nochlin, Anne Coffin Hanson, John Hollander, an artists' panel, and reminiscences by « Six Who Knew Edward Hopper, » pp. 115–160.

——. « Symbol and Reality in Edward Hopper's "Room in New York," » *Arts Magazine*, 56 (January 1982), pp. 148–53.

——. « In the Footsteps of Edward Hopper, » *Geo*, 5 (February 1983), pp. 36–45.

MORSE, John. « Interview with Edward Hopper, » *Art in America*, 48 (March 1960), pp. 60–63.

O'DOHERTY, Brian. « Portrait: Edward Hopper, » *Art in America*, 52 (December 1964), pp. 68–88.

SEITZ, William C. *Edward Hopper in São Paulo 9.* Washington, D.C.: Smithsonian Press, 1967.

ZIGROSSER, Carl. « The Etchings of Edward Hopper, » in *Prints*, edited by Carl Zigrosser. New York: Holt, Rinehart, and Winston, 1962.

LIST OF ILLUSTRATIONS

We wish to thank the owners of the pictures reproduced herein, as well as those collectors who did not want their names mentioned.

MUSEUMS

CHICAGO

The Art Institute.

LINCOLN, NEBRASKA

Sheldon Memorial Art Gallery.

MINNEAPOLIS

Walker Art Center.

PHILADELPHIA

Museum of Art.

NEW YORK

The Metropolitan Museum of Art – The Museum of Modern Art
Whitney Museum of American Art.

SAN FRANCISCO

The Fine Arts Museum.

WASHINGTON D.C.

Corcoran Gallery of Art – National Gallery of Art – National Portrait Gallery
The Phillips Collection

PRIVATE COLLECTIONS

Mr. and Mrs. Malcolm Chace – Mr. and Mrs. Barney A. Ebsworth – Mr. and Mrs. Albert Hackett – Mr. and Mrs. Joel Harnett – Mr. and Mrs. Gilbert H. Kinney – Loretta and Robert K. Lifton – Mr. and Mrs. Carl Lobell – The Sara Roby Foundation, New York – Mr. and Mrs. Frank Sinatra – Mr. and Mrs. Alvin L. Snowiss – Mr. and Mrs. Mortimer Spiller – The Thyssen Bornemisza Collection, Lugano, Switzerland - The Warner Collection of Gulf States Paper Co., Tuscaloosa, Alabama.

PHOTOGRAPHS

Geoffrey Clements, New York – Roy Elkind, New York – Eric Pollitzer, New York – The Hirschl and Adler Galleries, New York – The Kennedy Galleries, New York.